Happy Cooking!

IT'S SO GOOD

100 real food recipes for kids!

Welcome, Young Chefs!

When I was a little boy, visiting my grandparents was always a treat — and not just because they spoiled me with love and affection. My favorite part of the day was always the very early morning, just before sunrise. I would wake up with Gramma to help her in the kitchen. After walking down to the corner market for the newspaper and any necessary ingredients, she put me to work squeezing lemons, shelling peas or shucking corn.

Sitting down to eat later, I had a connection to the food we were enjoying and a sense of pride for having played a part in its preparation. Even though he's only eighteen-months-old, I'm already looking forward to teaching my son, Zephyr, the joys of putting a meal on the table.

Cooking is a skill that will serve you well throughout your life. Plus, it's a great way to learn about a lot of different subjects: math, science, social studies, and history. You may even learn how to speak a little French by using this cookbook!

No matter what you're making, always include a colorful variety of fruits and vegetables to create healthy, balanced meals. Fresh produce is best, but frozen or canned options work well, too. Keep an eye out for the strawberry icon – it indicates that at least two different types of fruits or vegetables are used in the recipe.

Now get cooking and have fun!

Nevin Martell
July 2014

© Kyle Martell

Always have an adult with you in the kitchen when preparing any of the recipes in this book.

CONTENTS

CONTENTS

Breakfast

Bacon, Egg, and Cheese Sandwich

© Piotr Rzeszutek - Fotolia.com

1 In a small pan, fry bacon or sausage on medium-high heat until it is cooked on both sides. Remove from pan and let rest on a plate covered by a paper towel to sop up the grease.

2 In the same small pan, on medium-high heat, fry the egg until the yolk starts to harden. Then flip the egg, place the two pieces of aged cheddar cheese on top of it, and cover the pan. Leave the pan on the stove for a couple more minutes, until the yolk has cooked through and the cheese has melted.

3 While the cheese is melting, split open your English muffin and toast it. When the egg is ready, put it on one of the English muffin halves. Salt and pepper to taste. Add avocado slices and/or tomato slices, if you like. Place second half of the English muffin on top and enjoy.

Serves 1

Ingredients

2 strips of bacon or
1 round breakfast sausage
1 egg
2 pieces of aged cheddar cheese
1 English muffin
Salt and pepper
½ an avocado, sliced (optional)
2 slices of tomato (optional)

TIP Feel free to slather on a little bit of your favorite condiment. Dijon mustard of sriracha sauce both work well.

Cinnamon Apple Oatmeal

©timolina - Fotolia.com

1 Combine oatmeal, water, apples, cinnamon, nutmeg, and clove in a saucepan.
Bring to a boil over medium-high heat, stirring occasionally. When it begins to boil, reduce the heat to a simmer and continue to stir occassionally. Let it simmer for 10 minutes or more until the oats are cooked through and the apple bits have softened.

2 Add dark brown sugar and mix together. You can add less sugar if your apples are very sweet or you want to reduce the overall sweetness. Spoon into bowls and serve warm.

Serves 1

Ingredients

2 cups (500 ml) oatmeal
3 ¾ cups (900 ml) water
3 apples cut into small pieces
½ teaspoon (2.5 ml) ground cinnamon
Dash of ground nutmeg
Dash of ground clove
¼ cup (60 ml) dark brown sugar

TIP Top off your bowl of oatmeal with chopped walnuts, and a splash of milk.

Raspberry Jam

1 Wash and drain the raspberries. Place them in a large saucepan and add the sugar, lemon juice, and water.

2 Cook over a low heat until the sugar has dissolved. Then continue cooking over a high heat, mixing well with a wooden spoon, for 15 minutes.

3 After 15 minutes, test if it is cooked by placing a few drops onto a cold plate. The jam is ready if it sets and forms a "pearl." If it spreads out over the plate, keep cooking for another 5 minutes.

Pour it into the jars, leave to cool, and cover.

Makes 4 jars

Ingredients

2⅓ lbs / about 9 cups (1 kg) of fresh or frozen raspberries
6 cups (1.2 kg) sugar
Juice of 1 lemon
¾ cup (180 ml) water

TIP If you prefer to make a jelly, pass the jam through a strainer to remove the seeds before transferring to the jars.

Hole in One

Serves 1

Ingredients

2 strips of bacon
1 slice of whole-wheat bread
1 egg
Salt and pepper

1 In a small pan, fry bacon on medium-high heat until it is lightly cooked on both sides.

2 Use a cookie cutter and cut a circular hole in the center of the whole-wheat bread (toast or fry it in the bacon fat). Place the bread on top of the two strips of bacon, which should be arranged parallel to each other like an equal (=) sign. Crack the egg into the hole, exposing the bacon strips.

3 Fry until the white has partially cooked through. Then flip the egg and bread over (the bacon should be fused to the bread by the egg). Let cook until the egg is done to your liking. Season with salt and pepper and eat warm.

TIP Use any shape cookie cutter that you want. Be creative!

9

Queen Muffins

© Johann Larson - Fotolia.com

Makes 8 muffins

Ingredients

¼ cup (30 ml) butter
⅓ cup (80 ml) sugar
1 egg
1 ½ (375 ml) cups flour
1 tablespoon (15 ml) baking powder
Pinch of salt

1 Pre-heat the oven to 400°F (200°C).

2 Cream together butter and sugar. Beat egg separately and then add to the butter-sugar mixture.

3 Sift together baking powder, flour, and salt. Add this dry mixture to the butter mixture, alternating with milk, until all three components are completely mixed. Fill the muffin trays three-quarters full.

4 Bake 20-25 minutes until golden brown on top. Turn out on to a cooling rack and leave to cool.

TIP To decorate your muffins, shake a little Demerara sugar onto the muffin batter before baking.

Pancakes

1 Place the flour, salt, and yeast in a mixing bowl.

2 Mix in the eggs with a wooden spoon and gradually add the milk, mixing constantly to avoid lumps from forming.

3 Once you have smooth batter, leave to rest for 1-2 hours.

4 Heat the oil in a non-stick frying pan. Pour into the pan, a ladle of batter, making a pancake about one-third of an inch thick. Cook until bubbles appear on the surface, and then turn it over and cook for another 1–2 minutes.

© Joshua Resnick - Fotolia.com

Serves 6-8
Ingredients

2⅓ cups (580 ml) of multi-purpose unbleached flour
Large pinch of salt
2¼ teaspoons (580 ml) of instant yeast
2 eggs
¾ cup milk (180 ml)
½ teaspoon (2.5 ml) vegetable oil

TIP You can top your pancakes with maple syrup, jam, or butter.

11

Bagel Faces

© klickerminth - Fotolia.com

Serves 1

Ingredients

1 whole-wheat bagel or bread
3 tablespoons (45 ml) plain or herbed
cream cheese
4 cucumber slices
1 tomato slice
2 small pieces of carrot

1 Cut the bagel in half and toast it. Spread the cream cheese evenly on both halves of the toasted bread.

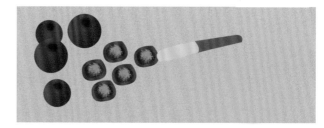

2 Place the cucumber rounds in the cream cheese to create eyes and ½ of the tomato slice below them to form the mouth. Place a carrot piece in between them as a nose.

 TIP Finely chop up some fresh chive to scatter below the tomato "smile" to give your Bagel Face a beard.

12

Granola with Berries and Yogurt

© Elena Elisseeva - Fotolia.com

Serves 4
Ingredients

8 oz (250 g) yogurt
3 tablespoon (45 ml) powdered sugar
1 cup (250 ml) strawberries
2 cups of raspberries (180 ml)
¾ cup (180 ml) blueberries
3 sprigs fresh mint
½ cup granola (125 ml)

1 Place the yogurt in a mixing bowl.

2 Wash and hull the strawberries then cut into 2 or 4 pieces. Rinse the raspberries and blueberries in cold water.

3 Wash the mint leaves and chop finely.

4 Into each serving bowl, put a layer of yogurt, then a layer of fresh fruit and mint, and top with granola.
Serve immediately.

Gramma's Cinnamon Rolls

© Viktoriya Biryukova - Fotolia.com

1. Pre-heat oven to 450°F (230°C). Sift together flour, baking powder, and salt.

2. Pour into a cup, but do no stir together, vegetable oil and milk. Pour all at once into flour and stir together with a fork.

3. Roll out dough to ¼-inch thickness. Spread with softened butter, brown sugar, and cinnamon. Roll dough up and cut into 1-inch thick rounds.

4. Place rounds flat on cookie sheet and cook for about 12 minutes, or until light golden brown.

Serves 4

Ingredients

2 cups (500 ml) all-purpose unbleached flour
1 tablespoon (15 ml) baking powder
1 teaspoon salt (5 ml)
⅓ cup (75 ml) vegetable oil
⅔ cup (160 ml) milk
3 tablespoons (45 ml) softened butter
½ cup (120 ml) dark brown sugar
2 teaspoons cinnamon

TIP Spread some well chopped walnuts over the dough before rolling it up to create crunch.

Waffles

Makes 12 waffles

Ingredients

⅓ cup (80 ml) butter
3 eggs
¼ cup (60 ml) milk
2 cups (500 ml) all-purpose unbleached flour
1 teaspoon (5 ml) baking powder
¼ cup (60 ml) sugar
Pinch of salt

1 Melt the butter in a saucepan over a low heat or in the microwave. Leave to cool.

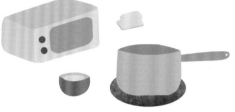

2 Beat the eggs in a large mixing bowl. Then add, a little at a time, the milk and flour, beating constantly to prevent lumps from forming.

3 Add the baking powder, sugar, salt, and cooled butter. Mix and leave to rest for 1 hour.

4 Heat a lightly oiled waffle machine. Pour in the batter using a ladle, and leave to cook for 1 to 2 minutes.

TIP Sprinkle a little powdered sugar on your waffles and enjoy!

© Dominik Tiziani - Fotolia.com

15

French Toast

© M.studio - Fotolia.com

Ingredients

2 eggs
1 cup (250 ml) milk
2 tablespoons (30 ml) sugar
8 slices bread
1 teaspoon (5 ml) vanilla sugar
3 tablespoons (45 ml) butter
Powdered sugar

1 In a bowl, beat the eggs. Pour the milk into a large shallow bowl, then mix in the sugar and vanilla sugar.

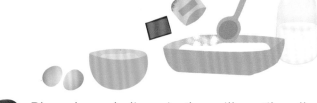

2 Place bread slices in the milk until well saturated, then dip both sides in the eggs.

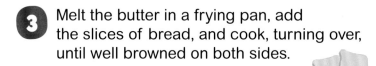

3 Melt the butter in a frying pan, add the slices of bread, and cook, turning over, until well browned on both sides.

4 Place the French toast on a plate and sprinkle a little powdered sugar on the top.

TIP You can also enjoy your French toast with maple syrup or jam.

Appetizers, Soups, and Salads

Cantaloupe
and Prosciutto

Serves 4

Ingredients

1 cantaloupe
12 thin slices of prosciutto
(Italian cured ham)

1 Slice the cantaloupe in half and scoop out the seeds with a large spoon.

2 Cut each half into three pieces and carefully remove the flesh from the skin with a knife.

3 Lay the cantaloupe slices on a serving tray. Add a slice of prosciutto between each slice of melon. Keep chilled until ready to serve.

TIP For a more eye-catching presentation, you can wrap pieces of cantaloupe in prosciutto and stick them on wooden or metal skewers.

© M.studio - Fotolia.com

Corn and Artichoke Salad

© Eric Pechin - Mond'Image

1 Bring a large pot of water to a boil. Submerge the asparagus and boil for 3 to 4 minutes. Drain and leave under cold running water to cool.

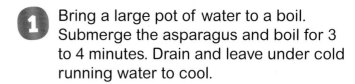

2 Cut the artichokes in half lengthways. Drain sweet corn and put to the side.

3 In a bowl, mix together the vinegar and salt, and then add the oils and pepper. In a tall glass, place half an artichoke heart, and put 4 asparagus around the side. Pour in the sweet corn, and then place the other artichoke half on top. Decorate with a few kernels of sweet corn.

4 Keep chilled until serving. Pour the salad dressing on just before serving.

Serves 4
Ingredients

1 bunch of asparagus
4 artichoke hearts
12 oz (341 ml) can of sweetcorn
1 teaspoon (5 ml) red wine vinegar
1 tablespoon (15 ml) olive oil
1 tablespoon (15 ml) vegetable oil
Salt and pepper

Tomato Gazpacho Soup

© Corinna Gissemann - Fotolia.com

Serves 4

Ingredients

8 ripe tomatoes
1 finely chopped clove of garlic
½ cup (125 ml) plain yogurt
2 tablespoons (30 ml) olive oil
Salt and pepper
8 chive sprigs

1 Wash, peel, and scoop the seeds out of the tomatoes. Cut the tomatoes into chunks, place in a blender and mix until puréed.

2 Add the garlic, yogurt, and olive oil to the blender. Mix again until smooth. Add salt and pepper to your liking.

3 Pour into a large bowl. Cover with plastic food wrap and place in the refrigerator.

4 Serve the tomato gazpacho in bowls. Decorate each bowl with 2 chive sprigs.

TIP Toasted slices of hearty country bread with cream cheese and chopped chives are a great accompaniment to your gazpacho!

Vegetable Soup

Serves 4

Ingredients

2 potatoes
3 carrots
1 onion
1 leek
1 turnip
1 large tomato
Salt and pepper

1 Wash and peel all the vegetables, and cut into small pieces. Cut the tomato into quarters and remove the seeds.

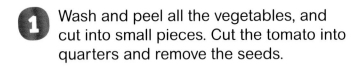

2 Place all the vegetables in a large saucepan. Add enough water to cover the vegetables. Cover and cook on a medium heat for about 30 minutes.

3 After it's cooked, remove the saucepan from the stove and blend until smooth. Season to taste.

TIP To give your soup a richer taste, simply add ½ tablespoon (7.5 ml) of cream as a garnish.

Carrot Soup

Serves 6

Ingredients

2.2 lb (1 kg) carrots
2 onions
4 cups (1 l) chicken stock,
vegetable stock or water
1 teaspoon (5 ml) sugar
1 tablespoon (15 ml) tomato purée
⅓ cup (80 ml) butter
Salt and pepper

1 Wash, peel, and slice the carrots. Peel and chop the onions.

2 Pour the stock into a large saucepan and add the carrots, onions, sugar, tomato purée, salt, and pepper.

3 Place a lid on the saucepan and cook for 40 minutes.

4 Take the pan off the heat. Blend the soup, add the butter, and season to taste. Serve hot.

 TIP Add 1 teaspoon curry powder to make a deliciously aromatic carrot soup.

© Bernd Jürgens - Fotolia.com

Bacon and Dandelion Salad

Serves 6
Ingredients

8 cups (2 l) of dandelion leaves
1 egg - 2 shallots
1 clove of garlic
8 slices of bacon, chopped into small pieces
1 tablespoon (15 ml) mustard
2 tablespoons (30 ml) balsamic vinegar
3 tablespoons (5 ml) olive oil
Salt and pepper - ½ cup (125 ml) cheddar
or Gruyere cheese cubes

1 Wash and dry the trimmed dandelion leaves.

2 Boil the egg in a pan of boiling water for 12-15 minutes. Rinse under cold water and remove the shell. Slice the egg. Peel and finely chop the shallots and the garlic.

3 Fry the bacon bits with a little oil in a frying pan. Once they are browned, remove from the heat and add to the salad bowl with the dandelion leaves.

4 In a bowl, mix together the mustard, vinegar, and olive oil. Add the chopped shallots and garlic, as well as salt and pepper. Pour over the salad and mix well. Decorate with the sliced egg and the diced cheese.

 TIP If you can't find dandelion leaves at your grocery store or local farmer's market, arugala works just as well.

Caprese Salad

Serves 4

Ingredients

⅔ lb (300g) fresh mozzarella
1 onion
4 large tomatoes
2 tablespoons (30 ml) balsamic vinegar
Salt and pepper
¼ cup (60 ml) olive oil
1 bunch of fresh basil

1 Cut the mozzarella and tomatoes into thin slices. Peel and finely chop the onion.

2 On a serving dish, arrange the tomato slices so they overlap one another. Then, place a slice of mozzarella between each of the tomato slices. Sprinkle the chopped onion over the top.

3 Mix together the salt, pepper, and balsamic vinegar in a bowl and mix well. Add the olive oil and mix again. Pour the dressing over the mozzarella and tomatoes.

4 Finally, add the finely chopped fresh basil leaves. Serve immediately!

TIP To add a little crunch to your tomato and mozzarella salad, add a few toasted pine nuts.

Radish and Zucchini Ribbons

© Chris Dave - Mond'Image

1 Rinse the zucchinis and radishes under cold water. Peel the grapefruit and cut into segments.

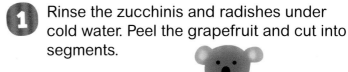

2 Using a vegetable peeler, make ribbons from the zucchinis, and thinly slice the radish. Place in a large salad bowl.

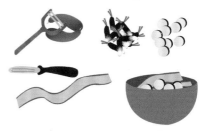

3 In a bowl, mix the balsamic vinegar, olive oil, salt, and pepper. Pour over the salad.

4 Decorate with the grapefruit segments and sprinkle on the cumin seeds. Serve immediately.

Serves 4

Ingredients

2 small zucchinis
12 radishes
1 grapefruit
1 tablespoon (15 ml) balsamic vinegar
2 tablespoons (30 ml) olive oil
Salt and pepper
1 teaspoon (5 ml) cumin seeds

TIP Only use the flesh of the zucchinis to make the ribbons.

25

Deviled Eggs

1 Boil the eggs for about 12 minutes. Rinse under cold water, remove the shell and slice in half lengthways.

2 Separate the yolks from the whites. Place the egg yolks in a bowl. Drain the tuna and flake into small pieces. Using a fork, mix the egg yolk, tuna, and mayonnaise.

3 On a serving tray covered with lettuce leaves, arrange the egg halves. Using a dessert spoon, divide the mix between the egg halves.

4 Sprinkle a little chopped parsley on top of each egg. Chill well before serving.

Serves 4

Ingredients

4 large eggs
6 oz (170 g) can of tuna
Mayonnaise
Chopped parsley
Lettuce leaves

TIP To decorate your deviled eggs, sprinkle a little paprika powder on each one.

© JJAVA - Fotolia.com

Italian Rice Salad

© Africa Studio - Fotolia.com

1 In a large saucepan, bring the water to the boil with a handful of salt and pour in the rice. Leave to cook for 10-12 minutes. When the rice is cooked, drain in a sieve and rinse under cold water. Add the butter.

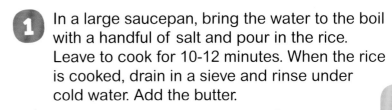

2 Wash the vegetables. Cut the tomatoes and eggplant into small cubes, and the peppers into thin slices.

3 In a frying pan, heat ¼ cup (60 ml) of the oil and fry the eggplant and peppers. Add salt and pepper. Add the rice, mix well and cook over a gentle heat for 7 minutes, stirring regularly.

4 In a large salad bowl, mix the balsamic vinegar with the dijon mustard, salt, pepper, and the rest of the olive oil. Add the rice and vegetables as well as the chopped tomatoes. Mix well and serve cold.

Serves 6
Ingredients

12 cups (3 l) water
¾ cup (430 ml) rice
2 tablespoons (30 ml) butter
4 tomatoes
2 tablespoons (30 ml) balsamic vinegar
2 tablespoons (30 ml) mustard
1 eggplant - 1 green pepper
1 orange pepper - 1 cup (250 ml) olive oil
Salt and pepper

Greek Salad

© cook_inspire - Fotolia.com

1 Wash the vegetables. Remove the seeds from the tomatoes, cucumber, and pepper and then dice them. Place everything in a large salad bowl. Add the olives and the feta, and mix.

2 Peel the onion and chop finely. Add to the salad.

3 Add the lemon juice and olive oil, then season with the oregano, salt, and pepper. Mix carefully and serve immediately.

Serves 4

Ingredients

2 large tomatoes - ½ cucumber
1 green pepper - 1 red pepper
⅓ cup (80 ml) green or black olives
1 cup (250 ml) feta cheese
1 large onion - Juice of ½ a lemon
2 tablespoons (30 ml) olive oil
1 teaspoon (5 ml) dried oregano

Potato Salad

© Studio Gi - Fotolia.com

1 Peel the potatoes and cook in boiling water for 10–15 minutes. When cool, dice, and then place in a salad bowl.

2 Dice the sausage and tomatoes, and then thinly slice the gherkins. Mix them all with the potatoes.

3 Put the cream, mayonnaise, and yogurt in a bowl. Add the salt and pepper and mix well. Add the sauce to the potato salad.

4 Chill before serving.

Serves 4
Ingredients

6 large potatoes
1 large Italian sausage, cooked
3 tomatoes
Small gherkins
1 tablespoon (15 ml) mayonnaise
1 tablespoon (15 ml) heavy cream
½ cup (125 ml) plain yogurt
Salt and pepper

Farmer's Chicken Salad

1. Cut the chicken breasts into small pieces and fry with a little butter. Once cooked, place the chicken in a salad bowl and leave to cool.

2. Wash, peel, and slice the apple. Place the apple and the cheese crumbles on top of the chicken.

3. In a bowl, mix the cream, mustard, oil, salt, and pepper. Keep the sauce in the refrigerator.

4. Pour the dressing on the lamb's lettuce and chicken, mix well. Garnish with the croutons.

Serves 4

Ingredients

2 chicken breasts - 1 tablespoon (15 ml) butter
1 apple - ¾ cup (180 ml) Roquefort blue cheese
2 teaspoons (10 ml) light cream
2 tablespoons (30 ml) mustard
3 tablespoons (45 ml) vegetable oil
Salt and pepper
½ cup (125 ml) plain croutons - Lamb's lettuce

TIP You can also make this recipe with Gruyere or cheddar cubes. Feel free to add a few walnuts, too!

© id1976 - Fotolia.com

Lentils and Grapefruit Salad

© Chris Dave - Mond'Image

Serves 4

Ingredients

1 cup (250 ml) dried lentils
2 tablespoons (30 ml) olive oil
1 tablespoon (15 ml) walnut oil
1 tablespoon (15 ml) balsamic vinegar
1 grapefruit
1 red onion
Small piece of feta cheese, diced
Basil leaves - Salt and pepper

1 Pour the lentils into a large pot of salted water and bring to a boil. Reduce heat and simmer for around 30 minutes.

2 Pour the olive oil, walnut oil, balsamic vinegar, salt, and pepper into a bowl. Mix well.

3 Peel the grapefruit and cut into segments. Peel the onion and slice.

4 Place the lentils in a large salad bowl, and pour over the dressing. Mix. Add the onions, feta, grapefruit segments, and basil leaves.

Endive Salad

© Chris Dave - Mond'Image

1 Carefully peel, wash, and drain the chicories. Cut the ham into ribbons.

2 In a salad bowl, mix the salt, pepper, mustard, and vinegar, then add the oil.

3 Add the walnuts to the salad dressing and stir well. Add the cheese cubes, ham, and chicory.

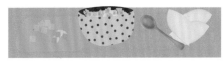

4 Mix the salad before serving to avoid bruising the chicory leaves. Cut a few stalks of chive over the top. It's ready!

Serves 4

Ingredients

4 endives
5 thin slices of ham
1 teaspoon (5 ml) Dijon mustard
2 tablespoons (30 ml) red wine vinegar
3 tablespoons (45 ml) olive oil
½ cup (125 ml) chopped walnuts
¾ cup (180 ml) diced Gruyere
or cheddar cheese
Chives - Salt and pepper

TIP You can also make this recipe with Gruyere or cheddar cubes. Feel free to add a few walnuts, too!

Main Course

Shrimp Skewers

Makes 8 skewers

Ingredients

1 red onion - 1 red pepper
1 yellow pepper - 2 small zucchinis
24 large shelled shrimps
6 cloves of garlic, finely chopped
2 shallots, thinly sliced
2 tablespoons (30 ml) olive oil
Juice of ½ a lemon - Salt and pepper

1 Peel the onion. Wash and cut the vegetables, including the onion, into large pieces. Assemble the skewers with 3 shrimp on each, alternating with the vegetables.

2 In a large dish, combine the olive oil and the lemon juice. Add the chopped garlic and shallots. Put the skewers in the dish. Cover with plastic food wrap. Place everything in the refrigerator for 30 minutes.

3 Cook the skewers on a grill, over a medium heat, for around 5 minutes. Turn regularly, until the vegetables are soft but still crunchy.

4 Leave to cool before serving.

TIP To make a tasty topping, add 2 tablespoons (10 ml) of the garlic and shallot marinade to mayonnaise.

© Kathleen Rekowski - Fotolia.com

Veggie Tabouleh

© Chris Dave - Mond'Image

1. Place the bulgur wheat in a large mixing bowl. Bring the water to a boil with a little salt. Pour on top of the grains and stir well. Cover and leave for 30 minutes.

2. Wash and dice the tomatoes and the cucumber. Finely cut the mint and parsley with a pair of scissors.

3. Drain the bulgur wheat and pour into a salad bowl. Squeeze the lemon juice over the bulgur wheat, pour olive oil to mixture. Add the diced tomatoes and cucumber as well as the chopped mint and parsley. Season with salt and pepper, and mix well.

4. Refrigerate for at least 2 hours before serving.

Serves 4
Ingredients

1 cup (250 ml) fine bulgur wheat
(or couscous) - ¾ cup (180 ml) water
2 medium tomatoes - ½ cucumber
1 bunch of fresh mint - 1 bunch of parsley
Juice of 3 lemons - ½ cup (125 ml) olive oil
Salt and pepper

Avocado with Shrimp

© lapsha_maria - Fotolia.com

Serves 6

Ingredients

3 avocados
½ lb (225 g) cooked and shelled shrimp
1 egg yolk
1 teaspoon (5 ml) mustard
¾ cup (180 ml) vegetable oil
Juice of 1 lemon
Parsley
Salt and pepper

1 Cut the avocados in half and remove the pits. Using a large spoon, scoop the flesh out of the avocados. Cut the flesh into cubes, and place in a mixing bowl with the shrimp.

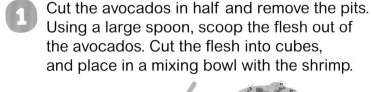

2 In a small mixing bowl, whisk together the egg yolk, mustard, and salt. Add the oil, a little at a time, whisking well before adding more. Once all the oil has been added, season and add the lemon juice.

3 Carefully combine the mixture with the avocado and shrimp. Add a little parsley.

4 To serve, fill the empty avocado shells with the shrimp mix, and decorate with a few parsley leaves.

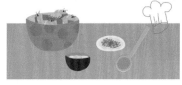

36

Vegetable Tartare

Serves 4

Ingredients

2 carrots - 2 small zucchinis - 2 spring onions
2 celery sticks - 10 radishes - 4 small tomatoes
1 tablespoon (15 ml) lemon juice
1 tablespoon (15 ml) vegetable oil
1 tablespoon (15 ml) flat parsley
½ cup (125 ml) plain yogurt
1 teaspoon (5 ml) mustard
1 tablespoon (15 ml) dill - Salt and pepper
8 lettuce leaves

1. Peel the carrots. Wash the zucchinis, onions, celery, tomatoes, and radishes. Finely dice all the vegetables.

2. Pour the lemon juice, yogurt, mustard, oil, and herbs into a large mixing bowl. Add the chopped vegetables, mix again, and season with salt and pepper.

3. Serve the vegetable tartare on a lettuce leaf.

Niçoise Stuffed Tomatoes

© JJAVA - Fotolia.com

1. Cut a "hat" (the top where the stem was once attached) off each of the tomatoes. Using a teaspoon, scoop out the insides of the tomato. Put what you've removed, including the juice, into a bowl.

2. Finely chop the basil. In a large mixing bowl, mix together the egg yolks and mustard, plus salt and pepper to taste. Slowly add the oil, a little at a time, whisking constantly to create mayonnaise.

3. Once that is ready, add the lemon juice and basil. Drain and flake the tuna, then mix with the basil mayonnaise. Using a spoon, fill the tomatoes with the tuna mix. Garnish the tomatoes with their "hats" and a basil leaf.

Serves 4
Ingredients

8 small firm tomatoes
Few fresh basil leaves
2 egg yolks
1 teaspoon (5 ml) mustard
⅓ cup (80 ml) vegetable oil
Juice of 1 lemon
6 oz (170 g) can of tuna
Salt and pepper

TIP To avoid the tomatoes rolling around on the plate, cut a thin slice off their bottoms.

Bacon and Eggs Pie

Serves 6

Ingredients

1 pre-made pie crust
6 slices bacon, cut into small pieces
4 eggs
2 cups (500 ml) light cream
Salt and pepper

1 Pre-heat the oven to 400°F (200°C).

2 Place pre-made pie crust in pie pan and puncture the pastry with a fork. Scatter the bacon bits over the crust. In a bowl, whisk together the eggs and cream with a fork. Add a little salt and pepper.

3 Pour this mix into the crust. Cook in the oven for 40 minutes or until the filling has cooked through and solidified. Serve hot with a green salad. Be careful not to burn yourself when removing the pie from the oven.

TIP You can add a little grated cheddar or Gruyere cheese to the eggs and cream mixture, which will add a yummy gooeyness.

© JJAVA - Fotolia.com

Whipped Carrots

Serves 4

Ingredients

1 bag of carrots
3 tablespoons (45 ml) butter
½ tablespoon (7.5 ml) chopped parsley
3 tablespoons (45 ml) cornmeal
3 tablespoons (45 ml) light cream
Salt and pepper
Chopped parsley

1 Wash and peel the carrots. Slice them into rounds. Cook for 20 minutes in boiling water.

2 Drain the carrots and blend in a blender or food processor.

3 Place a saucepan on a low heat and pour in the carrot purée. Add the butter. In a small bowl, mix the cornmeal with the cream until it has dissolved. Pour the liquid into the saucepan. Mix well and season with salt and pepper. Remove from the heat before it reaches boiling point.

4 Sprinkle with parsley and serve warm.

TIP If you want to thicken the purée without using cornmeal, you can add a large diced potato to the carrots.

© Chris Dave - Mond'Image

Crispy Crunchy Chicken Wings

© unpict - Fotolia.com

Serves 4

Ingredients

1 tablespoon (15 ml) vinegar
1 tablespoon (15 ml) cornmeal
⅓ cup (80 ml) sesame seeds
2 ⅔ cup (660 ml) plain breadcrumbs
1 egg white
¾ cup (180 ml) finely chopped walnuts
12 chicken wings
60 ml vegetable oil
Salt and pepper

1 Mix the sherry vinegar, cornmeal, walnuts, sesame seeds, and egg white in a bowl. Pour the breadcrumbs into another bowl.

2 Season the chicken wings with salt and pepper. Dip each wing into the first mix, and then coat in the breadcrumbs, rolling well to cover each side.

3 Pour the oil into a frying pan. When pan is hot add the chicken wings and fry each side for about one minute.

4 When cooked, drain the chicken wings on a paper towel. Serve immediately.

TIP These chicken wings go well with the carrot purée (see recipe on page 40).

Tuna and Tomato Tart

© sou52 - Fotolia.com

1 Pre-heat the oven to 400°F (200°C). Place pre-made pie crust in pie pan and puncture the pastry with a fork. Spread the mustard over the base.

2 Break the eggs into a bowl and mix with the cream. Add ½ cup (125 ml) of the grated cheese. Season with salt and pepper to taste.

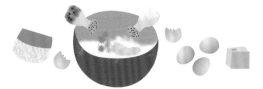

3 Drain and flake the tuna and spread over the crust. Rinse tomatoes, cut into thin slices, and place on top of tuna. Sprinkle the rest of the cheese on top and pour on the egg mix. Bake for 45 minutes.

Serves 6

Ingredients

1 pre-made pie crust
3 tablespoons (45 ml) Dijon mustard
4 eggs
1 ⅔ cup (410 ml) light cream
1 cup (250 ml) grated cheddar or Gruyere cheese
6 oz (1 x 170 g) can of tuna
2 tomatoes
Salt and pepper

TIP This dish tastes great served hot or cold. Add a salad for a filling lunchtime meal!

Hot Ham and Cheese Sandwich

1. Pre-heat the oven to 440°F (220°C). During this time, melt the butter in a saucepan. Add the flour and cook for 5 to 6 minutes, stirring well.

2. Pour the millk into the saucepan and bring the mixture to a boil, stirring well with a whisk. Remove from the heat and add the two egg yolks and half the grated cheese. Season with salt and pepper.

3. On an oven tray, place 8 slices of bread. On each of them, place half a slice of ham, a little grated cheese, another slice of bread, a spoonful of the mixture and finish off with more cheese. Bake in the oven for 15 to 20 minutes.

Serves 4

Ingredients

¼ cup (60 ml) butter
⅓ cup (80 ml) all-purpose unbleached flour
2 cups (500 ml) milk
2 egg yolks
1 cup (250 ml) grated cheddar or Gruyere cheese
16 slices of bread
8 slices of ham
Salt and pepper

TIP For a filling lunchtime meal, you can add a mixed salad!

Cantonese Rice

© Chris Dave - Mond'Image

1. In a saucepan, cook the rice according to the instructions on the package. Add the peas for the last 3 minutes of cooking.

2. Break the eggs into a bowl, season with salt and pepper and whisk well to create an omelet mixture.

3. Cook the omelet in a frying pan with a little butter. Once cooked, cut the omelet, as well as the ham, into thin slices.

4. Drain the rice and peas. Pour into a medium bowl, and add the strips of ham and omelet. Serve hot.

Serves 4
Ingredients

1¼ cups (310 ml) basmati long-grained rice
1 cup (250 ml) cooked shelled peas
3 eggs
2 slices of ham
Butter
Salt and pepper

TIP Serve in individual soup bowls.

Ham and Puréed Potato Parcels

© Chris Dave - Mond'Image

Serves 4

Ingredients

2 large baking potatoes
¾ cup (180 ml) milk
4 thin slices ham
Salt and pepper
Cooking strings

1 Peel the potatoes and cut in half lengthways, or into quarters for larger potatoes.

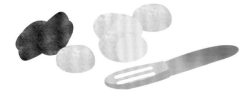

2 Bring the potatoes to a boil in salted water and cook for 15-20 minutes. Check they are cooked with the point of a knife.

3 Drain the potatoes and mash with a fork or potato masher. Incorporate the pre-heated milk little by little. Season with salt and pepper.

4 On a serving tray, lay out the slices of ham and place a small mound of mashed potatoes in the center of each one. Close the slices by tying a piece of cooking string around the top. Serve the rest of the mashed potatoes on the side.

Zucchini Flan

1 Pre-heat the oven to 440°F (220°C). During this time, wash the zucchinis. Cut into rounds without peeling. Chop the basil.

2 In a frying pan, heat the oil and fry the zucchinis. Add the salt, pepper, and basil. Leave to cool.

3 In a large mixing bowl, mix the egg yolks, eggs, cream, and milk. Beat together with a whisk and season.

4 Place pre-made pie crust in a pie pan. Spread the cold zucchinis over the base and pour on the egg mix. Bake in the oven for 25 minutes. Serve hot.

Serves 6

Ingredients

4 zucchinis
Few fresh basil leaves
1 cup (250 ml) milk
3 tablespoons (45 ml) olive oil
1 cup (250 ml) light cream
2 egg yolks
2 whole eggs
1 pre-made pie crust
Salt and pepper

TIP This zucchini flan makes a good side dish to serve with meat or fish.

© Mi.Ti. - Fotolia.com

Pasta Bolognese

Serves 4

Ingredients

1 large onion
1 ¼ cup (310 ml) chopped tomatoes
1 tablespoon (15 ml) dried mixed Italian herbs
2 tablespoons (30 ml) olive oil
1 ⅓ lb (600 g) ground beef
1 lb (450 g) spaghetti
Parmesan or Pecorino Romano cheese
Salt and pepper

1 To make the bolognese sauce, peel the onion and cut into thin slices. Fry gently with the olive oil for 1 minute.

2 Add the ground beef to the frying pan, season with salt and pepper, and cook, stirring regularly.

3 Once the meat is well browned, add the tomatoes and mixed herbs. Cover the pan and leave to simmer on a low heat, stirring occasionally.

4 During this time, cook the pasta in a large pot of boiling water, following the instructions on the package. Once the pasta is cooked, drain, and serve on a plate or in a bowl with the bolognese sauce on top. Finish it off with grated Parmesan or Pecorino Romano cheese.

© Viktor - Fotolia.com

47

Fish Gratin

1. Pre-heat the oven to 400°F (200°C). Peel the carrots and zucchinis, and cut into slices. Wash the leek and slice thinly. Peel and chop the onion.

2. Cook the vegetables in a frying pan with a little olive oil. Season and mix well.

3. In a baking dish, put half the vegetables in a layer. Add the fish fillets and cover with the rest of the vegetables. Pour the cream on top, add the grated cheese and cover with aluminium foil.

4. Bake for 15 minutes, then remove the foil and bake for another 10 minutes until golden brown.

Serves 4
Ingredients

3 carrots - 3 zucchinis
1 leek - 1 onion
1 tablespoon (15 ml) olive oil
4 frozen cod fillets
¾ cup (180 ml) light cream
½ cup (125 ml) grated cheddar
or Gruyere cheese
Salt and pepper

Ratatouille

1. Peel and finely chop the onions. Peel the zucchinis and the eggplants. Cut the pepper and remove the seeds. Finely chop the garlic and cut all the vegetables into small cubes, including the peeled tomatoes. Keep the vegetables separate from one another.

2. In a large saucepan, heat the olive oil and add the onions and peppers. Cook for 5 minutes.

3. Add the tomatoes and cook for 5 minutes, stirring occasionally.

4. Add the zucchinis, eggplants, and thyme. Cover and leave to simmer for 30 minutes over a low heat. When finished cooking, add the chopped garlic and seasoning. Serve hot.

Serves 4

Ingredients

2 onions
3 zucchinis
2 eggplants
2 peppers (1 red + 1 green)
4 cloves of garlic
28 oz (796 ml) can of tomatoes
1 sprig of thyme
3 tablespoons (45 ml) olive oil
Salt and pepper

Leek Quiche

Serves 4

Ingredients

3 large leeks
1 tablespoon (15 ml) olive oil
2 eggs
1 pre-made pie crust
¼ cup (60 ml) light cream
1 cup (250 ml) grated cheddar
or Gruyere cheese
Salt and pepper

1 Pre-heat the oven to 350°F (180°C). During this time, wash the leeks, remove the roots and cut into small slices.

2 Fry the leeks in a little olive oil for 30 minutes, stirring regularly.

3 In a large bowl, beat together the eggs with the cream, and add the salt and pepper.

4 Unroll the pre-made pastry in a tart dish and puncture with a fork. Spread the leeks over the pastry and pour the egg mix on top. Sprinkle on the grated cheese. Bake for 30 minutes and serve hot.

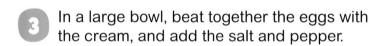

TIP For a tasty addition, put a few bacon bits into your egg mix.

Herb Omelet

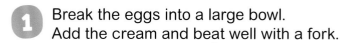

1. Break the eggs into a large bowl. Add the cream and beat well with a fork.

2. Add the ground tarragon, chives, and parsley to the eggs. Mix well.

3. Heat the oil in a frying pan over high heat. Once the pan is hot, pour in the egg mix and reduce the heat. Leave to cook for approximately 5 minutes.

4. Using a wooden spatula, lift the omelet occasionally to prevent it from sticking. Serve hot.

Serves 3

Ingredients

6 eggs
1 tablespoon (15 ml) light cream
Pinch of parsley
Pinch of chives
Pinch of ground tarragon
1 teaspoon (5 ml) olive oil
Salt and pepper

TIP Enjoy a tasty, fresh whole wheat bread and fresh tomatoes with your omelet.

Amazing Cheeseburgers

Serves 4

Ingredients

1 onion - 1 clove of garlic
1 tomato - 8 slices of cheddar cheese
4 burger buns
1 teaspoon (5 ml) dried mixed herbs
1 ⅓ lb (600 g) ground meat (beef or veal)
4 lettuce leaves
½ tablespoon (7.5 ml) vegetable oil
Salt and pepper

1. Pre-heat your oven to 350°F (180°C). During this time, finely chop the onion and garlic, and thinly slice the tomato.

2. By hand, mix the ground meat with the garlic, onion, and herbs. Add salt and pepper. Make 4 patties the size of the burger buns. Cook the patties in a frying pan with a little oil.

3. Slice open the burger buns and heat in the oven, for 1 minute. Remove from the oven and spread with your condiments of choice.

4. Assemble your burgers in this order: bread/cheese/meat/cheese/slice of tomato/lettuce leaf/bread. Put back in the oven for 2 minutes and then serve immediately.

TIP For a real treat, serve your cheeseburger with homemade fries!

Rainbow Hash

©Chris Dave - Mond'Image

1 Peel and grate all the vegetables. In a separate bowl, mix the egg and the flour. Add the grated vegetables, salt and pepper, then mix well.

2 Using your hands, press into thin patties and place onto waxed paper.

3 Heat the olive oil in a frying pan. The oil should be very hot. Add the hash to the frying pan. They are ready when golden brown all over.

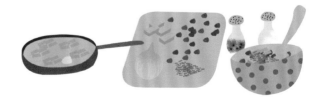

Serves 4

Ingredients

5 potatoes - 5 carrots
1 onion - 2 round zucchinis - 1 egg
3 tablespoons (45 ml) all-purpose unbleached flour
2 tablespoons (30 ml) olive oil
Salt and pepper

Margherita Pizza

Serves 4

Ingredients

1 ball of pizza dough or pre-made pizza crust
1 tablespoon (15 ml) olive oil
2 tomatoes
¼ lb (100 g) fresh mozzarella
2 sprigs fresh oregano
⅓ cup (80 ml) tomato sauce
¾ cup (180 ml) grated Parmesan cheese
Olive oil - Salt and pepper

1 Roll out the pizza dough to a large round and place on a lightly oiled oven tray. Drizzle a little olive oil on the dough. Pre-heat the oven to 400°F (200°C).

2 Wash and dice the tomatoes. Drain the mozzarella and cut into slices. Finely chop the oregano.

3 Spread a layer of tomato sauce over the dough and cover with diced tomatoes. Season with salt and pepper. Add the sliced mozzarella. Sprinkle with the oregano and Parmesan.

4 Place in the oven and bake for 30 to 35 minutes (cooking time may vary if you use a pre-made crust). Serve with a green salad.

TIP You can make many kinds of pizza with your favorite toppings, but always make sure to include the tomato sauce and chopped tomatoes!

Ham and Olive Loaf

1. Pre-heat the oven to 350°F (180°C). During this time, slice the olives and dice the ham.

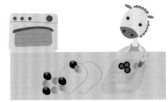

2. Into a large mixing bowl, sift the flour and baking powder. In another bowl, beat together the eggs, oil, and milk. Add a little salt and pepper. Pour on top of the flour and mix well.

3. Add the grated cheese and mix well. Add the ham and the olives. Mix again.

4. Pour into a greased and floured loaf tin. Bake for 50 minutes. Leave to cool before removing from the mold.

Serves 6
Ingredients

1 cup (250 ml) green and black pitted olives
2 thick slices of ham
1 cup (250 ml) all-purpose unbleached flour
2 teaspoon (10 ml) baking powder
4 eggs - 1 tablespoon (15 ml) olive oil
⅓ cup (160 ml) grated cheddar or Gruyere
⅓ cup (80 ml) milk - Salt and pepper

TIP The olives are naturally salty, so it's not necessary to add much salt to the mixture.

Potato Gratin

© azurita - Fotolia.com

1 Peel and finely slice the potatoes. Peel the garlic and rub it on the base of a large baking dish.

2 Pre-heat your oven to 350°F (180°C). During this time, in a large mixing bowl, beat together the eggs, cream, and milk.

3 Arrange the potato slices in the baking dish. Pour the cream mix on top and add salt and pepper.

4 Leave to cook for one hour. Remove from the oven, sprinkle the grated cheese on top and return to the oven for 15 minute until the cheese has browned.

Serves 6

Ingredients

3 lb (approx. 1.5 kg) potatoes
1 clove garlic
2 eggs
1 ½ cups (375 ml) light cream
¾ cups (430 ml) milk
⅔ cup (160 ml) grated cheddar
or Gruyere cheese
Salt and pepper

Ham and Cheese Croissants

© Brett Mulcahy - Fotolia.com

1 Pre-heat the oven to 350°F (180°C).

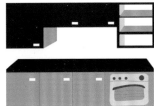

2 Cut the croissants in half lengthways. Spread the cream cheese on the inside of each croissant, then sprinkle on a little grated cheese.

3 Roll the slices of ham, place on the bottom half of the croissant and place the top half back on to close.

4 Place the croissants on a baking tray. Bake for 15 minutes and it's ready!

Serves 4

Ingredients

4 croissants
4 slices of ham
Cream cheese
Grated cheddar or Gruyere cheese
Salt and pepper

Shepherd's Pie

© azurita - Fotolia.com

Serves 4
Ingredients

2.2 lb (1 kg) potatoes
¼ cup (60 ml) milk
⅓ cup (80 ml) butter
1 onion - Parsley
1 lb (454 g) lean ground beef
19 oz (540 ml) can of creamed corn
¼ cup (60 ml) bread crumbs
Salt and pepper

1. Peel the potatoes and cut in half. Cook the potatoes in a pan of boiling water for 20 minutes. Drain.

2. In a bowl, mash the potatoes. Then, using a wooden spoon, add the milk and ¼ cup (60 ml) of softened butter to the mashed potatoes.

3. Peel and chop the onion. Cook in a frying pan with the rest of the butter. Add the beef and keep cooking until the meat is browned. Add the parsley and season with salt and pepper.

4. Pre-heat the oven to 440°F (220°C). Pour the meat into a baking dish, pour a layer of the creamed corn over the top, and then cover with the mashed potatoes. Sprinkle a layer of bread crumbs on top, and bake for 25 minutes.

Chili Con Carne

© CCat82 - Fotolia.com

1 Peel the garlic and onion then chop into small pieces. Wash the pepper, remove the seeds, and cut the flesh into small cubes. Rinse the kidney beans.

2 Heat the oil in a casserole dish on a low heat. Fry the onion and garlic for 2 minutes. Add the pepper and the ground beef. Cook for another 5 minutes, stirring regularly.

3 Add the beans, tomatoes, water, chili seasoning, salt and pepper. Stir well, cover, and leave to cook for 1 ½ hour.

4 Serve the chili in thick bowl to preserve the heat.

Serves 4

Ingredients

1 clove of garlic - 1 onion
19 oz (540 ml) kidney beans
½ green pepper
3 tablespoons (45 ml) olive oil
19 oz (540 ml) can of chopped tomatoes
¾ cup (180 ml) water
½ lb (200 g) lean ground beef
3 tablespoons (45 ml) chili seasoning
Salt and pepper

TIP White rice makes a great side dish for your chili con carne!

Beverages

Hot Chocolate

Serves 4

Ingredients

4 oz (120 g) dark chocolate
1 tablespoon (15 ml) water
4 cups (1 l) milk
4 teaspoons (20 ml) heavy cream

1 Break the chocolate into pieces in a saucepan. Add the water. Melt over a low heat.

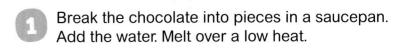

2 Once the chocolate has melted, add a little milk and mix well.

3 Gradually add the milk, mixing constantly. Make sure the milk and chocolate are well mixed before adding more milk.

4 Once the chocolate milk is hot, take it off the heat and remove the skin, which may have formed on top. Add the heavy cream and mix one last time.

TIP For a real gourmet hot chocolate, you can sprinkle cocoa powder or chocolate flakes on top and pop in a couple marshmallows.

Fruit Smoothie

© Printemps - Fotolia.com

Serves 2

Ingredients

1 large banana
Handful of frozen mixed berries
¾ cup (180 ml) orange juice
2 cups of milk (500 ml)
1 tablespoon (15 ml) sugar
Few ice cubes

1 Peel and slice the banana.

2 Place the sliced banana, berries, orange juice, milk, and sugar in a blender. Blend for a couple of minutes or until you have smooth mix.

3 Add the ice cubes and blend again until you have a thick mix.

4 Serve the smoothie in large glasses with a straw and drink chilled.

TIP To make a thicker smoothie, add a cup of plain yogurt.

Fruit Sangria

Serves 4

Ingredients

2 peaches
2 kiwis
2 apples
2 nectarines
2 oranges
8 cups (2 l) of grape juice
4 cups (1 l) of lemonade

1. Peel all the fruit. Dice the peaches, kiwis, apples, and nectarines, and cut the oranges into segments.

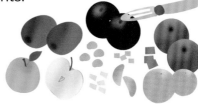

2. Pour the grape juice into the mixing bowl and add the fruit. Leave to sit overnight in the refrigerator.

3. Add the lemonade just before serving.

4. Using a ladle, pour the sangria into small goblets or glasses. Make sure each glass has fruit in it.

Spotted Pink Milkshake

© Christophe Valentin - Mond'Image

Serves 1

Ingredients

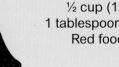

5 or 6 fresh strawberries
½ cup (125 ml) milk
1 tablespoon (15 ml) sugar
Red food coloring

1 Wash and hull the strawberries.

2 Mix the strawberries, milk, and sugar in a blender.

3 Pour the mixture into a tall glass.

4 Add a few drops of red food coloring to make the red spots.

TIP You can use ½ cup of yogurt instead of milk.

Banana Flip Flap Flop

© Christophe Valentin - Mond'Image

Serves 1

Ingredients

2 ice cubes
1 banana
½ cup (125 ml) of milk
½ cup (125 ml) of heavy cream
½ lemon skin, grated
(only the yellow part of the skin)
1 tablespoon (15 ml) sugar
1 tablespoon (15 ml) cocoa powder
1 egg yolk

1 Finely chop the ice in a blender.

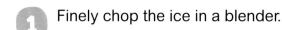

2 Peel the banana, cut it into circles and put them in the blender with the ice.

3 Add the milk, cream, egg yolk, lemon shavings, and the sugar. Mix it all together.

4 Serve your banana drink in a big glass with a straw. Sprinkle it with cocoa powder.

Minty Green Delight

© maxsol7 - Fotolia.com

Serves 1

Ingredients

1 teaspoon (15 ml) of mint extract
1 ½ cups (375 ml) lemonade
Few leaves of fresh mint
1 lime

1 Pour the mint extract into the bottom of a large glass.

2 Add the lemonade and mix well.

3 To decorate, drop one or two leaves of fresh mint into your glass.

4 Cut a slice of lime. Make an incision into the center of the slice, so that it sits nicely on the rim of your glass.

TIP You can serve your Minty Green Delight with ice cubes, or simply put the lemonade in the fridge before making your cocktail.

Coconut Delight

Serves 1

Ingredients

4 ice cubes
⅓ cup (80 ml) pineapple juice
2 tablespoons (30 ml) of coconut milk
Grated coconut
1 piece of pineapple for decoration

1 Put two ice cubes in a shaker, then pour in the pineapple juice and coconut milk.

2 Shake briskly.

3 Tip the contents of the shaker into a large glass with two ice cubes.

4 Sprinkle your glass with grated coconut and place a segment of pineapple on the rim.

Red Fruit Milkshake

Serves 1

Ingredients

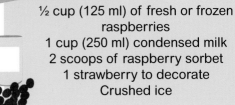

½ cup (125 ml) of fresh or frozen raspberries
1 cup (250 ml) condensed milk
2 scoops of raspberry sorbet
1 strawberry to decorate
Crushed ice

1 Put the raspberries, condensed milk, and raspberry sorbet in a blender. Mix together.

2 Pour your milkshake in a big glass with crushed ice.

3 Push a strawberry onto the rim of the glass for decoration and enjoy right away.

© CCat82 - Fotolia.com

Apple and Kiwi Compote

© Chris Dave - Mond'Image

Serves 4

Ingredients

4 apples
4 kiwis
2 tablespoons (30 ml) honey
1 teaspoon (5 ml) ground cinnamon

1 Peel and dice the apples and kiwis.

2 Place the fruits in a saucepan over a low heat. Add the honey and cinnamon, and cook for 25 minutes.

3 Purée the compote in a blender.

4 Pour the compote into glasses and refrigerate.

TIP Serve with mini shortbreads (recipe on page 92), which you can dip into the compote.

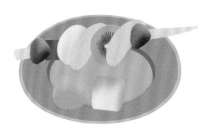

Snacks

Grapefruit Surprise

© Chris Dave - Mond'Image

Serves 4

Ingredients

2 grapefruits
½ lb (225 g) cooked shelled shrimp
3 oz (85 g) tins of tuna packed in water
2 tomatoes
2 avocados
2 tablespoons (30 ml) olive oil
Salt and pepper

1 Cut the grapefruits in half. Remove the flesh from the skins. Keep the grapefruit flesh as you will need it later for decoration.

2 Dice the avocados and the tomatoes, and mix together with the shrimp and drained tuna in a large salad bowl.

3 In a bowl, mix 1 tablespoon of grapefruit juice, squeezed from the flesh, with the olive oil, salt and pepper. Pour on top of the salad bowl ingredients and mix well.

4 Fill each half grapefruit with the tuna mix and decorate with grapefruit segments. Serve chilled on a few salad leaves.

Fruit Kebabs

© Monkey Business Images

1 Wash all the fruit.

2 Put the berries and marshmallows on the skewers, alternating between the different berries and the marshmallows.

Makes 16 kebabs
Ingredients

3 mixed cartons of your favorite fresh berries
Marshmallows
16 wooden skewers

Bruschettas

© M.studio - Fotolia.com

Makes
12 bruschettas

Ingredients

6 slices of ham
1 ⅔ cups (410 ml) tomato sauce
1 clove of garlic, chopped basil
12 pieces of baguette bread,
each about 3-4 inches long
2 balls of fresh mozzarella cheese
Olive oil

1 Pre-heat the oven to 350°F (180°C). In a bowl, mix the tomato sauce, chopped garlic, and chopped basil. Put the sauce aside.

2 Toast the pieces of bread in a toaster. Cut the ham and mozzarella into slices.

3 Peel the clove of garlic and rub it onto the pieces of bread. Add a dribble of olive oil to each slice and spread on the sauce.

4 Share the ham and mozzarella between the slices of bread. Put in the oven for 10 minutes. Serve your bruschettas either hot or warm.

TIP

To bring variety to your bruschettas, make them with other ingredients: goat cheese, Gruyere, tuna, diced bacon, chopped red pepper, whatever makes you happiest. The options are endless!

Sweet Popcorn

Serves 6

Ingredients

¾ cup (180 ml) kernels of popcorn
1 tablespoon (15 ml) of vegetable oil
Powdered sugar

1. Put the oil in a saucepan and cover the bottom of the inside pan with popcorn kennels. Mix with a wooden spoon.

2. Heat over a very low flame, covered with a lid (it's good if the lid is transparent so that you can see your corn pop).

3. Wait until the kernels stop popping before you turn off the stove and lift the lid.

4. Fill a large bowl with the popcorn and dust with powdered sugar.

Chocolate Pudding

Serves 6

Ingredients

6 egg whites
4 egg yolks
¼ cup (60 ml) of sugar
3 tablespoons (45 ml) of butter
8 oz (240 g) of dark chocolate
Powdered sugar

1 Put the butter and chocolate pieces in a mixing bowl. Melt for 4 minutes in the microwave.

2 In another mixing bowl, whip the egg whites with half the sugar. When they stiffen, add the rest of the sugar.

3 Mix the egg yolks into the melted chocolate. Delicately mix in the whipped egg whites. Butter the bottom of a mold and gently pour the mixture in. Cook for 4 minutes in the microwave.

4 Bring the pudding out of the microwave. Let it cool before taking it out of the mold. Place your cake on a plate and dust with powdered sugar.

SNACKS

TIP For an even more chocolaty taste, cover your chocolate pudding in chocolate icing. Melt 6.5 oz (200 g) of milk chocolate and ⅓ cup (80 ml) butter for 4 minutes in the microwave. It's a sweet finishing touch!

© Hetizia - Fotolia.com

Desserts and Baking

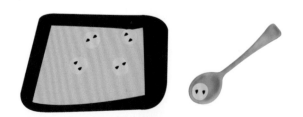

Fresh Fruit Salad

Serves 4

Ingredients

12 strawberries
20 raspberries
1 pineapple
1 kiwi
2 bananas
1 grapefruit
1 tablespoon (15 ml) fine sugar
or brown sugar

1 Wash the strawberries and raspberries. Peel the pineapple, kiwi, and bananas, and cut into pieces.

2 Peel the grapefruit and cut into thin slices.

3 In a salad bowl, mix together the chopped fruits, except the pineapple and grapefruit, and sprinkle the sugar on top. Mix.

4 Leave the fruits to absorb the sugar for 1 hour. Place in serving bowls and decorate with pineapple and grapefruits slices.

TIP To give your fruit salad a refreshing touch, add a few finely chopped mint leaves.

DESSERTS

Homemade White Bread

Makes 1 loaf
Ingredients

a bottle of milk
4 cups (1 l) all-purpose unbleached flour
2 teaspoons (10 ml) salt
2 teaspoons (10 ml) baking powder
1 teaspoon (5 ml) vegetable oil
¼ cup (60 ml) of warm water

1 Place the flour, salt, and baking powder in a large mixing bowl. Add the oil and water and mix to a smooth dough with a wooden spatula.

2 Sprinkle the countertop with flour. Knead the dough until you have a smooth and elastic dough (it should no longer stick to your fingers).

3 Roll the dough into a ball. Score the top with a knife. Cover with a tea towel (one used to dry dishes) and leave to rise.

4 Pre-heat the oven to 440°F (220°C). The dough is ready to bake when it has doubled in volume. Bake for 35 minutes. Leave to cool on a cooling rack before cutting.

TIP You'll know your bread is fully baked if it sounds hollow when you tap it!

Milk Bread

© A_Lein - Fotolia.com

Makes 1 loaf
Ingredients

2 cups (500 ml) bread flour
2 tablespoons (30 ml) sugar
1 teaspoon (5 ml) salt
4 teaspoons (20 ml) baker's yeast
¾ cup (180 ml) warm water
⅓ cup (80 ml) softened butter milk

1 Place the flour, sugar, and salt in a large mixing bowl. Make a well in the center and pour in the yeast, followed by the milk and the butter. Mix well with a wooden spoon to obtain a soft, smooth dough.

2 Place a tea towel over the bowl and leave the dough to stand for 15 minutes.

3 Roll the dough into a sausage shape, and place in a large cake tin. Cover with a tea towel and leave to rise for 45 minutes. Pre-heat the oven to 350°F (180°C).

4 Once the dough has risen, bake for 25 minutes, until the crust is golden brown.

TIP If you prefer small bread rolls, simply break up the dough into small smooth balls, giving them a slightly cylindrical shape.

Madeleines

© Jiri Hera - Fotolia.com

Makes 18
Ingredients

⅓ cup + 1 tablespoon (105 ml) butter
1 ¼ teaspoon (6 ml) baking powder
2 teaspoons (10 ml) warm water
3 eggs
½ cup (125 ml) sugar
1 cup (250 ml) multi-purpose unbleached flour
Madeleine baking tray(s) with molds to
accommodate 18 cakes

1 Pre-heat your oven to 460°F (240°C). Melt the butter in a saucepan.

2 Mix the yeast and water in a cup.

3 In a bowl, beat together the eggs and sugar until light and creamy. Add the flour, yeast mix, cooled butter, and mix well.

4 Lightly grease the molds with some butter in the baking tray and fill with the mix until each mold is three-quarter filled. Cook for approximately 20 minutes. If there is still some mix left, bake another batch.

TIP For a zesty kick, add grated orange or lemon peel to your mix.

Chocolate Chip Cookies

Serves 4

Ingredients

½ cup (125 ml) softened butter
½ cup (125 ml) sugar
1 teaspoon (5 ml) vanilla sugar
1 egg
1 cup (250 ml) all-purpose unbleached flour
1 teaspoon (5 ml) baking powder
⅓ cup (80 ml) chocolate chips

1 Pre-heat the oven to 375°F (190°C). In a bowl, beat together the softened butter with the sugar and vanilla sugar.

2 Add the egg, flour, baking powder, and chocolate chips. Mix well.

3 Lay a sheet of non-stick baking paper on the oven tray. Place small mounds on the tray, leaving plenty of space between them.

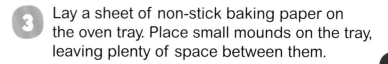

4 Bake for about 8 minutes. Don't overcook the cookies. They will be done when they're browned around the edges. Leave to cool slightly before eating.

TIP For extra crunch, add ⅓ cup (80 ml) of your favorite chopped nuts to your cookie dough.

Lemon Zest Cake

© cook-and-style - Fotolia.com

Serves 6

Ingredients

4 eggs
⅓ cup (80 ml) butter
1 cup (250 ml) sugar
½ lemon skin, grated
(only the yellow part of the skin)
1 ½ cups (375 ml) all-purpose unbleached flour
1 teaspoon (5 ml) baking powder

1 Pre-heat your oven to 350°F (180°C). Separate the egg whites and egg yolks into two bowls. Whisk the egg whites to soft peaks. Put to one side.

2 Melt the butter in a saucepan over a low heat or in the microwave.

3 In a large mixing bowl, beat together the egg yolks with the sugar. Add the lemon shavings, flour, baking powder, and melted butter. Carefully fold in the whisked egg whites.

4 Grease a loaf tin. Pour in the cake mix and bake for 45 minutes. Remove from the tin and leave to cool before eating.

TIP To make sure your cake is thoroughly baked, insert the point of a knife, which should come out clean.

Chocolate Truffles

© Brent Hofacker - Fotolia.com

Makes 30

Ingredients

13 oz (400 g) dark chocolate
½ cup (125 ml) butter
3 egg yolks
1¼ cups (310 ml) light cream
1 ¾ cups (430 ml) powdered sugar
¾ cup (180 ml) cocoa powder

1 Put the chocolate and butter, broken into pieces, in a saucepan. Melt on a very low heat.

2 Remove the saucepan from the heat. Pour the melted chocolate into a mixing bowl, and gradually add the egg yolks, cream, and powdered sugar. Mix well between each ingredient. Place in the fridge and chill for 3 hours.

3 Scoop out small pieces of batter and roll between your fingers to form a ball.

4 Place the cocoa in a bowl, and roll the truffle balls until lightly coated. Keep the truffles chilled until ready to serve.

TIP To spice it up, mix ½ teaspoon of ground cinnamon with the cocoa powder before you roll the balls in it.

Cheese Cake

1. Mix cream cheese, ⅔ cup sugar, eggs, and ½ teaspoon vanilla until smooth. Pour into well greased 9-inch pie plate.

2. Bake 22 to 25 minutes at 350 °F (180°C). Turn oven off. Remove cheesecake and cool for 5 minutes.

3. Mix in 3 tablespoons sugar, and remaining vanilla. Spread over warm cheesecake and return to oven for 5 minutes.

4. Cool and refrigerate.

Serves 4
Ingredients

2 packages (8 oz each) (250 g) cream cheese, softened
⅔ cup sugar
3 large eggs
½ teaspoon vanilla (2.5 ml)
3 tablespoons sugar (45 ml)
8 oz sour cream (250 g)

TIP For the perfect finishing touch, add a strawberry or cherry purée!

DESSERTS

Chocolate Muffins

1 Pre-heat the oven to 350°F (180°C). Place paper cups in the muffin trays.

2 In a large mixing bowl, mix together the flour, oil, light brown sugar, and baking powder. Add the milk, eggs, and vanilla. Mix again.

3 Add the chocolate chips and the cocoa powder. Mix lightly – the dough should look slightly lumpy.

4 Fill the muffin trays three-quarters full. Bake for 20 minutes. Turn on to a cooling rack and leave to cool.

Makes 12 muffins
Ingredients

2 ⅓ cups (580 ml) all-purpose unbleached flour
¼ cup (60 ml) vegetable oil
⅓ cup (80 ml) light brown sugar
2 teaspoon (10 ml) baking powder
1 cup (250 ml) milk
2 tablespoons (30 ml) cocoa powder
½ cup (125 ml) chocolate chips
1 teaspoon (5 ml) vanilla sugar
2 eggs

Crêpes

Serves 4

Ingredients

1½ cups (375 ml) all-purpose unbleached flour
2 eggs
2 tablespoons (30 ml) vegetable oil
1 pinch of salt
1 teaspoon (5 ml) vanilla sugar
2 cups (500 ml) milk

1 Pour the flour into a large mixing bowl. Make a well in the center and pour in the eggs, oil, salt, and vanilla sugar. Mix with a wooden spoon.

2 Pour in the milk, a little at a time, stirring constantly, until you have a smooth batter. Leave to rest for 1 hour.

3 Place the frying pan on a medium heat, and oil slightly. When hot, pour in half a ladle of the crêpe batter. Tip the frying pan so that the batter coats the base of the pan.

4 When the crêpe is starting to color, slide a spatula under the crêpe and flip it over. Leave to cook for another 30 seconds, then slide the crêpe onto a plate.

TIP If your batter still has a few lumps in it, remove them by passing it through a sieve.

Chocolate Marble Cake

© Printemps - Fotolia.com

Serves 6

Ingredients

3 eggs, separated
⅓ cup (80 ml) sugar
1 cup (250 ml) all-purpose unbleached flour
2 teaspoon (10 ml) baking powder
3 tablespoons (45 ml) butter
½ cup (125 ml) cocoa powder
Butter for greasing
Pinch of salt

1 Beat together egg yolks and the sugar. In a mixing bowl, combine the flour and baking powder. Add the butter (softened in the microwave) a little at a time, followed by the egg whites.

2 Whisk the egg whites with a pinch of salt until soft peaks form, and fold into the flour mix. Pour half of the dough into another bowl, and then add the cocoa powder. Mix.

3 Pre-heat the oven to 350°F (180°C). Grease a loaf tin and fill with alternate layers of the plain dough and the cocoa dough.

4 Once the tin is full, cover with a piece of aluminum foil and cook for 1 hour. Remove from the tin while hot. Serve warm or cold.

DESSERTS

Walnut and Almond Brownies

Serves 6

Ingredients

6 oz (200 g) unsweetened chocolate
½ cup (125 ml) butter
¾ cup (180 ml) water
3 eggs
¾ cup (180 ml) sugar
⅓ cup (80 ml) all-purpose unbleached flour
⅔ cup (160 ml) chopped walnuts

1 Pre-heat the oven to 400°F (210°C). In a saucepan, melt the chocolate, butter, and water on a very low heat.

2 In a mixing bowl, beat together the eggs and the sugar. Add the melted chocolate. Then, mixing well, add the flour a little at a time.

3 Add the walnuts to the dough and mix carefully.

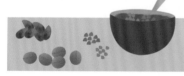

4 Grease a rectangular baking dish. Pour in the dough and bake for 20 minutes. Leave to cool before cutting into small squares.

© hanabiyori - Fotolia.com

Mini Cakes

Serves 10

Ingredients

1 cup (250 ml) plain flour
1 teaspoon (5 ml) baking powder
¼ cup (60 ml) butter
¼ cup (60 ml) sugar
2 eggs
½ cup (125 ml) plain yogurt
¼ cup (60 ml) chopped candied fruit

1 Pre-heat the oven to 400°F (200°C). In a bowl, mix the flour and baking powder.

2 Place the butter and sugar in a large mixing bowl. Mix smooth with a wooden spoon. Add 1 egg and half the flour mix. Mix well. Add the other egg and the remaining flour. Incorporate the yogurt and dried fruit and mix again.

3 Fill buttered individual cake molds three-quarters full with the dough. Bake for 15 to 20 minutes. Check the cakes are thoroughly baked by inserting a toothpick: it should come out clean. Leave to cool for 5 minutes before removing from the molds.

Flan Tart

Serves 8

Ingredients

4 eggs
¾ cup (180 ml) finely ground sugar
⅔ cup (160 ml) cornmeal
2 teaspoon (10 ml) vanilla sugar
4 cups (1 l) milk
1 sheet pre-rolled puff pastry (½ lb / 230 g)

1 In a large mixing bowl, beat together the eggs and half the sugar. Add the cornmeal and the vanilla sugar. Mix thoroughly.

2 In a saucepan, heat the milk and the remaining sugar. When it boils, add to egg and cornmeal mix, stirring constantly.

3 Place the mix back in the saucepan on a low heat, stirring constantly until it starts to thicken. Remove from the heat.

4 Unroll the puff pastry, place in the bottom of a deep tart dish and puncture a few times with a fork. Pour in the custard mix. Cook your flan for about 40 minutes at 350°F (180°C).

TIP If you add a few squares of semi-sweet chocolate to the milk, you'll have a delicious chocolate flan!

© sebalaphoto5 - Fotolia.com

Apple Pound Cake

Serves 6

Ingredients

2 or 3 baking apples
(such as Granny Smith or McIntosh)
1 cup (250 ml) sugar
¾ cup (180 ml) melted butter
4 eggs
1 ½ cups (375 ml) all-purpose unbleached flour
2 teaspoon (10 ml) baking powder

1. Pre-heat the oven to 350°F (180°C). Peel the apples and cut into thin slices. Arrange the apple slices in the bottom of a greased cake tin.

2. In a large mixing bowl, beat together the sugar and melted butter. Add the eggs one by one, and finally add the flour and baking powder. Mix well.

3. Pour the cake mix on top of the apples in the cake tin. Bake for approximately 30 minutes.

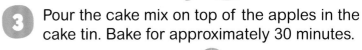

4. Check to see if the cake is cooked with the point of a knife. If the cake starts to brown on top before being cooked in the middle, you can cover it with aluminium foil.

TIP You can glaze your pound cake by pouring caramel on top of the apples. To make the caramel: heat ½ cup (125 ml) of sugar with a little water until it turns into a golden brown syrup.

DESSERTS

Shortbreads

© Christian Pedant - fotolia.com

Serves 6

Ingredients

2 cups (500 ml) all-purpose unbleached flour
½ cup (125 ml) sugar
1 egg
1 teaspoon (5 ml) baking powder
3 tablespoons (45 ml) milk
Few drops of vanilla extract
and orange flower extract
⅓ cup (80 ml) melted butter

1. Pre-heat the oven to 350°F (180°C).

2. In a large mixing bowl, combine the flour, sugar, egg, baking powder, milk, vanilla, orange flower extract, and melted butter. Knead the dough with clean hands.

3. On a clean countertop, roll out the dough with a rolling pin. Using various cookie cutters, cut out different shapes in the dough.

4. Place the shapes on baking paper and bake for 15 minutes.

TIP Enjoy these shortbreads with a big glass of cold milk or a delicious homemade hot chocolate (recipe page 61).

Swiss Roll

© Christian Pedant - Fotolia.com

Serves 8
Ingredients

4 eggs
½ cup (125 ml) sugar
¾ cup (180 ml) all-purpose unbleached flour
1 teaspoon (5 ml) baking powder
Jam of your choice
2 tablespoons (30 ml) butter
Pinch of salt
Powdered sugar

1 Pre-heat your oven to 400°F (210°C). Separate the egg whites and yolks. In a large mixing bowl, beat together the egg yolks and the sugar. Add the flour and the baking powder. Mix well with a whisk.

2 With an electric whisk or mixer, beat the egg whites with a pinch of salt until stiff peaks form. Fold into the rest of the mix, using a large spatula.

3 Grease an oven tray or square cake tin. Pour in the cake mix and spread out evenly. Bake for 10 minutes.

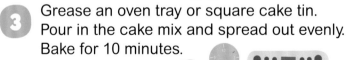

4 Sprinkle powdered sugar over your countertop. Carefully remove the cake from the tin onto the powdered sugar. Spread a layer of the jam on the cake and roll.

TIP You can also replace the jam with chocolate spread or Nutella.

Chocolate Sauce

Serves 8
Ingredients

5 oz (150 g) dark chocolate
5 oz (150 g) milk chocolate
2 tablespoons (30 ml) of water
⅓ cup (80 ml) 15% fat cream

1 Break the chocolate into a saucepan. Add two tablespoons of water.

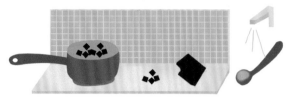

2 Melt the chocolate on a very low heat. Take the pan off the heat and add the cream. Mix carefully.

3 Return the chocolate to the stove and cook on a low heat for 5 minutes more.

4 You can serve the sauce with the Fruits Kebabs (see the recipe on page 72).

Peach and Cream Cheese Nutcake

© A_Lein - Shutterstock.com

Serves 6
Ingredients

2 cups (500 ml) all-purpose unbleached flour
1 cup (250 ml) ground almonds
⅔ cup (160 ml) sugar
⅔ cup (160 ml) butter
18 oz (250 g) packet of cream cheese
2 tablespoons (30 ml) of cornmeal
¼ cup (60 ml) milk
3 eggs - Pinch of salt - 6 peaches

1. Pre-heat the oven to 350°F (180°C). In a mixing bowl, mix flour, ground almonds, salt and ⅓ cup (80 ml) sugar. Add ⅓ cup (80 ml) soft butter.

2. Spread your mixture into a greased mold. Puncture it with a fork and cook for 10 minutes in the oven.

3. Mix the rest of the sugar with the cream cheese. Dilute the cornmeal with the milk and add the eggs. Incorporate this mixture with the cream cheese. Put in the rest of the melted butter and mix well.

4. Tip what you have prepared on top of your pre-cooked cake mixture. Wash the peaches and cut them into quarters. Place them on the cake and bake for 30 minutes.

TIP This cake tastes just as delicious if you use pears instead of peaches!

DESSERTS

Fruits of the Forest Charlotte

Serves 6
Ingredients

2.2 lb (1 kg) of fresh or frozen summer fruits
¼ cup (60 ml) of powdered sugar
Juice of ½ a lemon
1 cup (250 ml) of whipped cream
60 sponge finger cookies or ladyfingers
1 teaspoon (5 ml) orange juice

1 Whisk the cream until it forms stiff peaks. Wash and clean the summer fruits.
In a food mixer, mix 1 ½ lb (800 g) of summer fruits, the sugar and the juice of ½ a lemon. Mix. Then, mix in with the whipped cream (but save a bit for the finishing touches).

2 Dip the ladyfingers in the orange juice diluted with 1 teaspoon (5 ml) of water. Line the bottom and sides of the charlotte mold with doused ladyfingers.

3 Alternate layers of fruit cream and layers of sponge fingers, finishing with a layer of sponge fingers. Put your charlotte in the fridge for at least 3 hours.

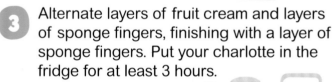

4 Once you have taken the charlotte out of its mold, decorate it with the rest of the fruit and a few small touches of whipped cream.

DESSERTS

Orange Chocolate Chip Cake

© Asia Yakushevich - Fotolia.com

Serves 4

Ingredients

½ cup (125 ml) plain yogurt
1 ½ cups (375 ml) unbleached all-purpose flour
1 cup (250 ml) of sugar
6 oz (180 g) of milk chocolate
3 eggs - 2 teaspoons (10 ml) of baking powder
1 teaspoon (5 ml) vanilla extract
1 orange skin, grated (only the orange part
of the skin) - ⅓ cup (80 ml) vegetable oil
2 tablespoons of butter

1 Pre-heat the oven to 350°F (180°C).
Put the yogurt, flour, and sugar in a mixing bowl.

2 Mix together. Add the baking powder, eggs, vanilla, orange shavings, and the oil.
Mix again vigorously.

3 Grate the chocolate and fold it into the mixture.

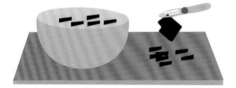

4 Grease a cake tin and pour in the mixture.
Put in the oven to bake for 25 minutes.

DESSERTS

Cherry Surprise

1 Pre-heat the oven to 400°F (200°C).

2 In a large mixing bowl, mix the flour, salt, and sugar. Beat the eggs and add to the mixing bowl. Pour in the milk, stirring constantly, until you have thick batter.

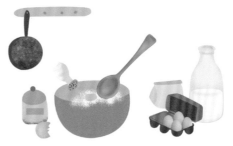

3 Pour the batter into a tart tin. Bake for 10 minutes.

4 Remove the tin from the oven and scatter the pitted cherries over the batter. Cook for another 30 minutes. Serve while still warm.

Serves 6
Ingredients

¾ cup (180 ml) all-purpose unbleached flour
Pinch of salt
¾ cup (180 ml) sugar
4 eggs
1 ⅔ cups (410 ml) milk
2.2 lb (1 kg) pitted cherries

TIP Frozen cherries can be substituted for freshly pitted cherries.

© Jérôme Rommé - Fotolia.com

DESSERTS

Crème Brulée

Serves 4

Ingredients

2 cups (500 ml) light cream
1 teaspoon (5 ml) vanilla extract
5 eggs
¼ cup (60 ml) finely ground sugar
4 teaspoons (20 ml) light brown sugar

1 Pre-heat the oven to 210°F (100°C). In a saucepan, heat the cream with the vanilla extract.

2 Break the eggs into a large mixing bowl and add the finely ground sugar. Beat together. Pour the hot cream on to the eggs, whisking constantly.

3 Pour the mix into 4 bowls that can be used in an oven. Bake in the oven for 30 minutes.

4 Sprinkle on the light brown sugar (1 teaspoon/5 ml per bowl) and place the dishes under a hot grill to caramelize the sugar.

DESSERTS

Chocolate-Icing Cakes

© ChantalS - Fotolia.com

Serves 6

Ingredients

8 oz (250 g) dark chocolate
1 cup (250 ml) butter
7 eggs
1 cup (250 ml) sugar
¾ cup (180 ml) all-purpose unbleached flour
Butter and flour for the bowls to be baked

1 Pre-heat the oven to 350°F (180°C). Melt the chocolate and butter in a saucepan on a very low heat.

2 Vigorously beat the eggs and the sugar, until you have a light creamy mousse. Carefully mix in the melted chocolate and add the flour a little at a time, mixing well.

3 Pour the mix into small buttered and floured bowls that can be used in an oven.

4 Cook for 8 to 10 minutes. Carefully remove from the bowls and serve immediately.

TIP Serve your Chocolate-Icing Cakes with a scoop of vanilla ice cream. The hot and cold combination is irresistible!

Orange Tartlets

Serves 4

Ingredients

½ lb (230 g) pre-made pastry dough
3 oranges + 2 for decoration
¼ cup (60 ml) sugar
1 tablespoon (15 ml) cornmeal
3 eggs
1 small pat of butter

1 Pre-heat the oven to 350°F (180°C). Grease 4 individual tart tins. Line with the pre-made pastry dough and puncture with a fork. Blind bake the pastry cases, for 20 minutes by covering with baking paper and dried beans, and finish off with 5 minutes uncovered.

2 Squeeze 3 oranges and strain the juice. Take half the juice and mix in the cornmeal. Pour the rest of the juice into a saucepan and add the cornmeal. Heat gently, then add the cornmeal and juice. Stir.

3 Beat the eggs in a large mixing bowl, then add to the saucepan. Increase the heat and whisk constantly until it has thickened.

4 Pour the orange cream into the tartlet cases. Peel the oranges and slice thinly. Place on top of the tartlets and serve immediately.

DESSERTS

Little Pink Mousse

© asab974 - Fotolia.com

Serves 4

Ingredients

3 eggs
2 tablespoons (30 ml) sugar
2 teaspoons (10 ml) cornmeal
¾ cup (180 ml) milk
1 ¾ cups (430 ml) fresh or frozen strawberries
Pinch of salt

1 Separate the egg whites and the yolks. Beat the egg yolks with the sugar, and cornmeal. The mix should be light and creamy.

2 Gently heat the milk. Pour on to the egg yolks and mix well. Pour the liquid back in the saucepan and cook, stirring constantly, until thick. Transfer to a bowl.

3 Wash and hull the strawberries. Blend and mix with the other ingredients.

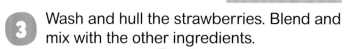

4 Whisk the egg whites to soft peaks with a pinch of salt. Refrigerate for a minimum of 2 hours.

TIP To serve your mousse, decorate with a few strawberries cut in half.

Chocolate and Caramel Bananas

© tashka2000 - Fotolia.com

1 Pour the sugar into a saucepan. Place on a low heat. Stir until the sugar starts to caramelize. Add the butter and remove from the heat.

2 Peel and slice the bananas. Divide between 4 dessert dishes.

3 In a second pan, melt the chocolate over a low heat.

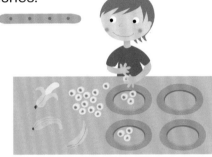

4 Pour the caramel over the bananas followed by the melted chocolate. Delicious!

Serves 4
Ingredients

¾ cup (180 ml) sugar
1 small pat of butter
4 bananas
3 oz (90 g) dark or milk chocolate

TIP Sprinkle a few almond slivers on top of your bananas for crunch.

DESSERTS

Apple Tart

Serves 4

Ingredients

½ cup (125 ml) all-purpose unbleached flour
⅓ cup (80 ml) sugar + 2 tablespoons (30 ml)
to garnish
Pinch of salt - 3 eggs
¼ cup (60 ml) milk
3 large apples - 1 tablespoon (15 ml) butter

1. In a large mixing bowl, mix the flour, ⅓ cup (80 ml) of sugar and the salt. Beat the eggs and add to the flour while mixing. Gradually add the milk, stirring well.

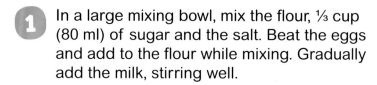

2. Pre-heat the oven to 350°F (180°C). Peel the apples and remove the seeds. Cut into thin slices.

3. In a frying pan with a little butter, lightly caramelize the apples. Arrange the caramelized apples slices so they overlap one another in a tart tin. Pour the batter on top.

4. Bake for 45 minutes. Sprinkle the remaining sugar on the cake and serve warm.

Peach Berry Salad

Serves 4

Ingredients

2 peaches
1 cup (250 ml) strawberries
1 cup (250 ml) blueberries
¼ cup (60 ml) sugar
1 cup (250 ml) raspberries
1 lime

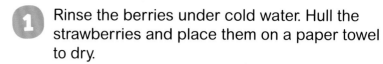

1. Rinse the berries under cold water. Hull the strawberries and place them on a paper towel to dry.

2. Cut the strawberries in half. Cut the peaches in half, remove the pits and cut into small cubes.

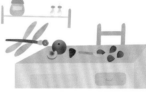

3. Place the fruits in a salad bowl and squeeze the lime juice on top.

4. Sprinkle sugar on your salad. Place in the fridge. Serve chilled soon after preparation.

TIP You can also put kiwis in your salad!

Coconut Milk Rice Pudding

© nanthapa - Fotolia.com

Serves 4

Ingredients

¾ cup (180 ml) coconut milk
¾ cup (180 ml) milk
2 tablespoons (30 ml) sugar
⅓ cup (80 ml) short-grain rice (e.g. Arborio)
1 vanilla pod
4 teaspoons (20 ml) shredded and dried coconut
1 mango cut into 8 slices

1 Heat the milk, coconut milk, rice, and sugar in a saucepan on a low heat.

2 Cut the vanilla pod in half lengthways, scrape out the seeds with the back of a knife and add to the pan.

3 Cook for 20 minutes, stirring regularly. Pour the rice pudding into 4 serving bowls. Refrigerate for 1 hour.

4 When you wish to serve the dessert, sprinkle with some dried coconut and place two slices of mango on each bowl.

TIP You can replace the mango slices with small pieces of pineapple.

DESSERTS

Pear and Chocolate Tart

Serves 6

Ingredients

1 pre-made pie crust
⅓ cup (80 ml) soft butter
1 cup (250 ml) ground almonds
½ cup (125 ml) sugar
2 eggs
3 oz (90 g) dark chocolate
3 pears
1 small pat of butter

1 Pre-heat the oven to 420°F (220°C). Place pre-made pie crust in a pan and puncture with a fork.

2 In a large bowl, mix the butter, sugar, and almonds until smooth. Beat the eggs and add to the mix.

3 Melt the chocolate in the microwave, about 4 minutes, then spread the chocolate on the pie crust. Add the almond mix on top of the chocolate.

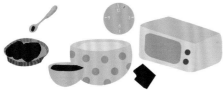

4 Cut and thinly slice the pears lengthways, and place on top of the tart. Cook the tart in the lower part of the oven for approximately 30 minutes.

Kiwi Surprises

© Viktorija - Fotolia.com

Serves 4

Ingredients

12 kiwis
1 ½ cups (375 ml) plain yogurt
3 tablespoons (45 ml) sugar

1. Cut off one end of each kiwi. Of the remaining three-quarters, carefully scoop out the flesh with a teaspoon.

2. Finely dice the flesh.

3. In a large bowl, mix together the yogurt and the sugar, add the diced kiwis and mix well.

4. Fill the kiwis with the yogurt mix and decorate with the remaining kiwi pieces. Serve chilled.

TIP You can serve your Kiwi Surprises with some delicious madeleines (recipe on page 80).

Almond Blondies

Serves 4

Ingredients

1 ½ cups (375 ml) all-purpose unbleached flour
1 teaspoon (5 ml) baking powder
½ teaspoon (2.5 ml) salt
⅓ cup (80 ml) butter
1 cup (250 ml) sugar - 2 eggs
1 teaspoon (5 ml) vanilla extract
½ cup (125 ml) toasted almond slivers
3 ½ cups (875 ml) fresh raspberries
Powdered sugar

1 Pre-heat the oven to 350°F (180°C). In a bowl mix until smooth the flour, baking powder, and salt.

2 Place the butter and sugar in a mixer for 3 minutes. Add the eggs and the vanilla, mix again. Add the flour and half the almonds, and mix to a smooth paste.

3 Transfer the mix to a greased square cake tin. Place the raspberries on top. Bake for 55 to 60 minutes.

4 Leave to cool. Sprinkle the rest of the almonds and the powdered sugar on before serving.

TIP Almond blondies taste great with a scoop of lemon sorbet.

DESSERTS

Tiramisu

© M.studio - Fotolia.com

1 In a large bowl, beat together the eggs, egg yolk, and sugar. Beat in the mascarpone.

2 In a bowl, prepare the milky coffee with four tablespoons of cocoa powder, mix well. Soak ladyfingers in the coffee mix. Place a layer of the ladyfingers on the bottom of a dish.

3 Cover with a layer of the mascarpone cream, then alternate layers of soaked ladyfingers and cream, finishing with a layer of the cream.

4 Refrigerate for at least 8 hours. Sprinkle on a layer of cocoa powder and grated chocolate just before serving.

Serves 8
Ingredients

3 whole eggs
1 egg yolk
½ cup (125 ml) sugar
8 oz (250 g) mascarpone cream
1 package ladyfinger cookies
1 strong coffee with milk
⅓ cup (80 ml) cocoa powder
Grated chocolate

TIP You can prepare your tiramisu in individual little jars or rammekins.

DESSERTS

Raspberry Sorbet

Serves 6

Ingredients

1 ½ lb / approx. 6 cups (700 g) fresh
or frozen raspberries
¾ cup (180 ml) fructose or sugar that
has been blended in a mixer
Juice of 1 lemon
¼ cup (60 ml) water

1 Blend 1 lb (454 g) of the raspberries in a blender until smooth.

2 Add the sugar, lemon juice, and water. Mix well and pour into a container.

3 Leave to set in the freezer for at least 2 hours.

4 Serve the sorbet in scoops with the remaining raspberries sprinkled on top.

TIP You can substitute fresh or frozen strawberries to make a tasty sorbet!

DESSERTS

© Doris Heinrichs - Fotolia.com

Chocolate Delight in a Mug

Serves 6

Ingredients

¼ cup (60 ml) milk
4 oz (125 g) dark chocolate
⅓ cup (80 ml) water
⅓ cup (80 ml) sugar
3 tablespoons (45 ml) cornmeal
1 egg
2 tablespoons (30 ml) butter
1 teaspoon (5 ml) orange blossom water

1 Heat the milk in the microwave for 2 minutes. Break the chocolate into pieces, place in a saucepan with the water, and melt on a low heat. Stir well to make a thick cream. Add the hot milk and stir well.

2 In a large bowl, combine the sugar and cornmeal. Add the egg and mix well, then gradually pour in the hot chocolate milk, stirring well before adding more.

3 Pour the mix into the saucepan and thicken over a low heat, whisking constantly. Remove as soon as it begins to boil.

4 Take off the heat, add the butter in small pieces and the orange blossom water. Pour the hot mixture into 6 mugs or small serving bowls. Chill for at least 6 hours, they should be firmly set.

TIP Add a sprinkling of cinnamon powder on top of your dessert for some added flavor!

Apple Crumble

© anjelagr - Fotolia.com

Serves 6
Ingredients

6 apples
Juice of 1 lemon
1 teaspoon (5 ml) ground cinnamon
1 cup (250 ml) all-purpose unbleached flour
1 cup (250 ml) light brown sugar
½ cup (125 ml) butter

1 Peel the apples and remove the seeds. Cut into large pieces. Spread over the base of a greased baking dish. Add the lemon juice and cinnamon.

2 In a large bowl, mix together the flour and sugar. Add the softened butter in small pieces. Using your hands, rub the butter into the flour until the mix resembles breadcrumbs.

3 Pre-heat the oven to 400°F (210°C). Cover the apples with the crumble mix, taking care not to leave any spaces.

4 Cook in the hot oven for 50 minutes. The topping should be browned and the apples soft.

TIP You can make your crumble with lots of other kinds of fruit! Try berries or pears – whatever suits your mood!

DESSERTS

Poached Pears

© M.studio - Fotolia.com

Serves 6

Ingredients

4 cups (1 l) water
1 cup (250 ml) sugar
6 Bartlett pears
Juice of 1 lemon
6.5 oz (200 g) dark chocolate
3 tablespoons (45 ml) butter
Vanilla ice cream

1 Pour the water and sugar into a large saucepan. Bring to the boil and reduce the heat. This will create a thick syrup.

2 Peel the pear, without removing the stem. Squeeze a little lemon juice on the pears. Immerse in the syrup on a low heat for 20 minutes. Leave to cool in the syrup.

3 In another saucepan, melt the chocolate on a very low heat. Add the butter and about ¼ cup (60 ml) of the pear syrup.

4 On each plate, place one pear, a scoop of vanilla ice cream and cover with the chocolate sauce. Serve immediately.

TIP To check that the pears are thoroughly cooked, cut into them with the point of a knife – they should be soft and slightly translucent.

Chocolate Mousse

Serves 4

Ingredients

6.5 oz (200 g) dark chocolate
4 eggs
Pinch of salt
Few almond slivers

1 Break the chocolate into a heat-proof bowl. Place it on top of a pan of hot water (the bowl should be touching the water). Melt the chocolate while mixing well with a spatula. Remove from the heat and leave to cool slightly.

2 Separate the egg yolks from the whites. Beat the egg whites with a pinch of salt to soft peaks. Add the yolks to the melted chocolate and mix.

3 Carefully fold the whisked egg whites into the chocolate mix, folding the mix from the bottom over the top.

4 Pour the chocolate mousse into 4 bowls and decorate with the almond slivers. Leave in the fridge for at least 2 hours before serving.

DESSERTS

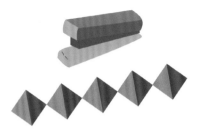

Kitchen
Projects

Frosted Glasses

You will need

1 glass
Grenadine syrup
Powdered sugar
2 saucers

1. Put a layer of powdered sugar in one saucer and grenadine syrup in the other.

2. Press the rim of your glass in the grenadine syrup, and then in the sugar. Put your glass in the refrigerator.

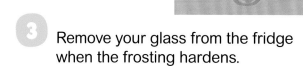

3. Remove your glass from the fridge when the frosting hardens.

4. To change the color, use different syrups.

TIP Use these glasses to serve Fruit Sangria (recipe page 63) or the Minty Green Delight (recipe page 66).

KITCHEN

Decorative Lanterns

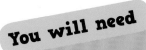

You will need

Scissors
String
Rectangular colored paper
Scotch tape
Stapler

1 Take a piece of colored paper and paint on colored stripes lengthways.

2 Fold the paper several times along its length, until it folds like an accordion.

3 Make snips in the folded edges. You can vary the shape of the snips.

4 Unfold the paper. You've made a Chinese lantern! Staple the two sides together. Fasten the two ends of the piece of string onto the lantern with Scotch tape. Hang up your lantern to decorate your home or your garden!

KITCHEN

Fancy Ice Cubes

© Jenny Sturm - Fotolia.com

1 Place a small fruit in each ice cube hole.

2 Fill the tray with water.

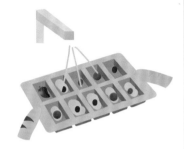

3 Put your ice cube tray in the freezer, for at least 2 hours.

4 Put an ice cube in each glass to go with the drink of your choice.

You will need

1 ice cube tray
Berries (blackberries, raspberries, blueberries) or other fruit diced into small pieces
Water

Rainbow Streamers

© Annaïs Tassone

You will need

Colored crêpe paper
Stapler
Scissors

1. Cut two strips of two different colors of crêpe paper.

2. Place the ends one over the other, and staple together at a right angle.

3. Fold one strip over the other, over and over again, braiding the streamer until you reach the end.

4. Secure the end of your streamer with staples.

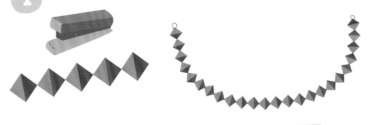

KITCHEN

TIP You can hang your streamer or use it to wrap gifts!

120

INDEX

INDEX